THE UNTAMED COAST

Other Books by Peter Jenkins

Along the Edge of America

Close Friends

Across China

The Tennessee Sampler (with Friends)

The Road Unseen

The Walk West

A Walk Across America

THE UNTAMED COAST

Pictures and Words
About Rare People and Rare Places
Along the Edge of America

Peter Jenkins

Rutledge Hill Press
Nashville, Tennessee

Published in Nashville, Tennessee, by Rutledge Hill Press, 211 Seventh Avenue North, Nashville, Tennessee 37219. Distributed in Canada by H. B. Fenn and Company, Ltd., Mississauga, Ontario.

Design by Harriette Bateman, Bateman Design, Nashville, Tennessee.

Color separations by Palace Press, Singapore.

Library of Congress Cataloging-in-Publication Data

Jenkins, Peter, 1951–
       The untamed coast : pictures and words about rare people and rare places
    along the edge of America / Peter Jenkins.
            p.   cm.
       ISBN 1-55853-347-8 (hardcover)
       1. Gulf Coast (U.S.)—Pictorial works.   2. Gulf Coast (U.S.)—Descrip-
    tion and travel.   3. Boats and boating—Gulf Coast (U.S.).   4. Jenkins, Peter,
    1951–   —Journeys—Gulf Coast (U.S.).   I. Title.
    F296.J465   1995
    976—dc20   95-38102
                                                                    CIP

Printed in the United States of America.

1 2 3 4 5 6 7 8 9—99 98 97 96 95

To my loving mother

Mary Robie Jenkins

who taught her children to see the beauty in our world, whether it be in a tiny wildflower, an unusual face, on a high hill, or across an ocean in a foreign land.

I love you, Mother, with all my heart.

Contents

Introduction

A few years ago I thought that my adventuring days were over. Taking risks that called for physical challenge, extreme mental demands, and the intense questioning of my soul, such as walking across America, was for my twenties and thirties. At the time I had about a year remaining in my thirties. That year, Brooke, one of my sometimes sweet, sometimes funny daughters gave me a black coffee mug with the slogan Over the Hill. I pretended to think it was funny, but the thought of my being over the hill was terrifying.

I realize now, almost five years later, how stupid that limiting, defeatist, pathetic thinking was. How could I have let that slow me down, stop me from seeing more of the world, discovering more of its astounding people, learning more about myself and who I am?

During this dark time I assumed that there was one adventure I would never have. I consoled myself that I'd already had enough excitement and discovery for a lifetime, more than anyone else I knew. The thing I wanted to do most was not a trip to somewhere, but a trip to anywhere as long as it was in a boat. Seeing some part of the world and finding it from a boat was a dream that had sparked me

on and off for as long as my mind held any memories. And so I decided that, yes, I would make this boat trip happen. No, I was not ready to be over the hill; I was nowhere near the summit.

Probably the most thrilling part of traveling, as in many rushes in life, is in the thinking about it. I considered many voyages. Should I go around Australia? No. That was too demanding for someone like me with no boating experience. Too far from home. The Atlantic Coast? The Pacific? The Mississippi? No. They all called to me, but not intensely.

The Gulf Coast. Yes, that was where I should explore. I would begin at the tip of the Florida Keys and go to the southern Texas border. How overwhelming the idea was. How thrilling. What a rush. I could do it. No, I couldn't. I could or sink trying. If I sank, I would fix the boat and keep going.

What kind of boat would I use? Should I travel in a kayak, a sailboat, a motorboat? Would I need a crew or could I do this alone? First, I chose as my home on the water a twenty-five-foot-long Grady-White Sailfish. It would be powered by two Yamaha outboard motors. In the world of boating, this type of vessel is called a sports fishing boat.

My boat, which I named the *Cooper,* could go under most bridges if I wanted to go any distance upriver. It could float in less than two feet of water, which meant I could pull up to a barrier island and plant the bow on the beach. I could head offshore thirty, even fifty miles, and handle any of the boat-bashing conditions the Gulf could deliver up. I could sleep aboard this boat. It even had a tiny cold shower. There was also an extra bunk so that my family would have a place to sleep whenever they joined me.

I had wanted to bring along a small kayak, but there was no room to lash it down and still travel at full cruising speed. So I settled on an inflatable that could be stowed on the boat. When I needed it, a foot pump would expedite its preparation. It needed only a few inches of water to float, and this would allow me access to the swamps and marshes and tight spots where the *Cooper* couldn't go. Many of the best pictures I took for this book were taken from my seven-foot-long Achilles inflatable.

Speaking of pictures, people who know my work think of me as a writer. My degree, however, a bachelor of fine arts, is in art and sculpture. When I walked across America I was very fortunate to make connections with *National Geographic* magazine. They loaned me a basic Nikon camera, then called a Nikkormat, a couple of lenses, and all the color slide film I could use. Since I had to carry all my photographic equipment in my backpack, I did not load myself down but carried as little as I could.

This experience taught me to do more photograph-ically with less, and that philosophy has been the basis for my approach to preserving in pictures the world I explore. I use as little equipment as I can. I don't use filters or motor drives, just a few lenses and a single camera body. This has worked well for me, although at times I've missed some incredible photographic opportunities because I did not have a certain lens, a specific filter, or a motor drive.

The pictures in this book were taken with a Nikon FM2 camera body and four lenses: a 28mm, an old and dented 105mm, and two telephoto lenses—a 180mm and a 300mm. All my film was Kodak slide, at least 95 percent of it ASA 64.

Probably the greatest lesson I learned about photography from the gifted people at *National Geographic* was what Tom Smith, former head of illustrations, told me more than once. Typically, he would offer this lecture after I had told him a story about some experience, such as my attending a three-hour service in an African American church. He would ask if I took any pictures, and I'd say no, that I was too overwhelmed by the experience, that I hadn't even thought of taking pictures.

Tom said that there was a big difference between photographers and writers. Writers can experience life, people, and places. They can pay attention or just go about living and years later dredge back up what they saw. Photography was different. Life had to be captured as it happened. Sometimes that moment lasted less than a second. He said that I had to pay exacting attention to what was happening each time something caught my attention. A tear trickling down a face. A vicious wind blowing you into hiding. A sunset that almost forces you to your knees in some kind of worshipful state. These dramatic, sometimes gentle, often just curiosity-arousing moments happen only for a moment, an instant. Sky colors may fill your eyes for only a few minutes, darkening, lightening, leaving.

I used to think rare people and rare places would reoccur, but they never do in exactly the same way. Tom told me that I had to be in the world I was experiencing and above it, looking down, analyzing the moment, determining if I should be recording it on film.

There were times on this voyage along the Gulf Coast, up its rivers, into its wetlands, that so excited me visually that I shot hundreds of pictures in fifteen minutes. Such moments seized me many times, like the extraordinary late afternoon at the beach and in the dunes at Gulf Shores, Alabama, when I took more outstanding (for me) pictures in an hour's time than I had ever before. One became the cover shot for *Along the Edge of America,* my written account of this journey; several others are in this book. Yet there were more times on this two-year journey that I did not take any pictures for days.

Of the many life-altering lessons I learned while walking across America, one of the most valuable was that to understand a place I had to linger there, live with its people, become consumed by the places they call home. To find these places, to be able to stop and stay, I have learned the rare art of wandering. I have asked many friends if they have ever wandered. Most look perplexed and say no. Wandering, being open like a sponge to everything around us, is something few of us do.

Wander I did, beginning in the Florida Keys, for two years. I knew this journey held many of America's most attractive and exotic places and people. What I knew drew me to the Keys, the Everglades, New Orleans, the Mississippi River, the Cajuns, and (God forgive me for not mentioning it first) Texas. These places ended up holding me to them for months at a time, as did places I'd never heard of before: the Ten Thousand Islands, the Jungle Woods, the rare white sands of the Florida Panhandle, Wilcox County (Alabama), wildlife-loaded Cameron Parish (Louisiana), the sand land that juts into Galveston Bay, and Seadrift (Texas).

I can never explore a place without being consumed by its people. In *The Untamed Coast* you will meet many inspiring people, ones often overlooked in our world. Certain people changed me forever because of their lives powered with courage and inspired by love. These rare people will speak to you in their own words. They are extraordinary people, such as Scott Bannerot, Billy and Red Parker, Daisy Durante, Minnie Leah Purdue, Debbie Therriot, Ralph Holmes, Judge Jackson, and Diane Wilson.

In my opinion, we focus too much attention on what is wrong and tragic in our world. Please come with me as we begin in the Florida Keys and voyage together for more than twenty-five hundred miles through a world where the focus will be on the inspiring.

The Florida Keys

An enchanting, beautiful world of water, sky, and little bits of islands begins south of Miami, at the beginning of the end of the Florida Peninsula. Known as the Keys, this loosely linked string of islands extends south and west for more than two hundred miles. Some are connected by seemingly endless bridges, others, like the Dry Tortugas, are reachable only by boat or floatplane.

All life on and around the Keys is extraordinary, exotic. The bird life is unlike anywhere else in the country. More than six hundred varieties of fish fill the surrounding waters. Some are smaller than my hand and so vividly colored they excite the brain as they swarm by. Of course, the area is also home to sharks large enough to swallow a person in two bites. Sea turtles the size of coffee tables paddle around in water so clear that on a good day swimmers can see the turtles fifty feet beneath them.

People have an amazing ability to adjust to most environments. Those who call the Keys their home are so accustomed to an unusual freedom to pursue their individuality that living elsewhere and conforming to a larger group is unheard of.

The color of the water and the sky makes the area extraordinary. There are only little bits of land for humans and other land creatures to cling to. The Keys are a priceless necklace of jewels along the edge of America. A treasure for everyone.

Ospreys hunt the surrounding waters for fish. This one returns to its nest in a young mangrove tree. *Florida Bay, near Lower Matecumbe Key.*

Scenes like this are not uncommon. A former seaworthy craft is left for the water to claim. Today it provides a perch for some water birds and underwater protection for smaller fish and crustaceans. *Florida Bay, near Islamorada.*

As well traveled as I am, I have never seen so many overwhelmingly intense colors anywhere as I saw in the Keys in one sunset. This one began as mostly blue; the center of the sky was an intense, yet soft yellow. The colors changed to electric orange, then orange red, then solid pink, then a deep purple before darkening to a black like polished marble. *Florida Bay, near Long Key.*

This twenty-five-foot boat, the *Cooper,* was my home off and on for two years. After snorkeling or free diving in the glass-clear waters of the Keys on a clear-sky day, the cold shower on board felt excellent. Following an evening meal of boiled lobster or some other seafood, the waves would often rock me to sleep. *Florida Bay, near Big Pine Key.*

When not at his home port of Mobile, Alabama, Warren Norville (above) would prefer to be roaming the Keys, a place where he can be free to let his adventurer's heart loose.

On the way to the Dry Tortugas, one of the most awesome and seldom seen places in the United States, I came upon this antique lighthouse (left). It once helped keep mariners from wrecking on the Marquesas Keys. *Near Satan Shoal.*

With a wingspan of up to ninety inches, what the man-o'-war bird does best is fly. The species is also known as a frigate bird. John J. Audubon thought them to be one of the most elegant and spectacular of all flyers. This one was hovering over a hunting sailfish, hoping the larger fish would scare a few flying fish into breaking the surface. Man-o'-wars can catch the furtive fish in midair. *Off Islamorada.*

Man-o'-wars (below) roost in the mangrove islands around the Keys. They are certainly not graceful landers, having to tuck in their long, long wings. A great blue heron (center) also checks in for the night. *Florida Bay, near Lower Matecumbe Key.*

Keys lobsterman Kenny Hildebrant (left) glances back at his trap line to make sure he didn't miss any of the bright orange buoys that mark his lobster traps. It is February in the Keys and time to gather the traps and store them for the next lobster season. Kenny, a former homebuilder from New Jersey, came to the Keys more than fifteen years ago to fish. He was instantly enchanted by the nonconformist water world and determined to some day return to this 200-mile string of coral reefs and keys. Now, like many longtime Keys residents, he and his wife feel that the lifestyle that first attracted them has been changed irrevocably by too much community growth and too many new people. *Florida Bay, near Yellow Shark Channel.*

In the Keys, where every square inch of ground is precious and where zoning laws increasingly control what can be done, storing lobster traps becomes a bigger and bigger challenge. At one time, these clumps of traps were a kind of local kitsch, but now more affluent newcomers see them as eyesores. These traps (near right), however, make fine perches for lounging pelicans. *Lower Matecumbe Key.*

Kenny (far right) holds up one of the last spiny lobsters of the season. These lobsters lack the meaty claws of Maine lobsters, but their tail meat is at least as succulent and delicious. This lobster and several more were my pay for helping Kenny haul in his traps. Several traps had been damaged beyond repair by sea turtles who tore the wooden slates apart to feast on the trapped lobsters. Trigger fish also get into the traps for an easy meal. Unfortunately, recreational divers steal many lobsters, too.

This mature brown pelican lives around Windley Key. Every day as the charter fishing boats return to port, this bird flies to meet each, hoping the deck hands will feed it any leftover baitfish. The fishermen always oblige. *Outside Holiday Isle.*

After a long day of diving in search of small fish, these cormorants gather on some guide wires. *Florida Bay, near Seven Mile Bridge.*

Anchored in the Keys and all around the Gulf Coast are sailors who wander from port to port. They cruise from brash and rowdy port cities like Houston, New Orleans, and Tampa to bays so isolated that the loudest noise is that of a mullet breaking the surface of the still waters. *Summerland Key.*

Many skills are needed to run a successful charter fishing boat. You have to know how to read the ocean and its infinite moods. You have to know about the hundreds of species of fish you seek to catch. Some prowl just beneath the surface of the water. Some live deep, amid the rocky shelf. Some migrate through certain areas during specific weeks of the year. Some live under the shadows of buoys. There is so much to know. One of the most important things to know, however, is how to throw a sixteen-foot-diameter net, which Kenny (left) holds. With it, you can catch live bait, the first necessity for sport fishing. *Off Plantation Key.*

A sailfish leaps in a futile attempt to throw a hook. This one fought for almost thirty minutes before being brought alongside to be tagged and released.

SCOTT BANNEROT has for as long as he can remember been drawn to the exotic world that is South Florida. He earned a doctoral degree in marine biology from the University of Miami, but the academic life was not for him. When I met him, he had made yet another dream of his come true: he was a charter fishing captain of his own boat. As I write this, Scott is pursuing yet another dream—he and his wife are sailing around the world in their sailboat, the *Elan*. They may spend five years on the voyage, or twenty; they may never return.

While I lived on my boat in the Keys I went out on many charters with Scott. Some days the clients were so hung-over or so seasick that I got to fish in their place.

On such a morning I was in Scott's boat headed to a fishing place called the Hump, an undersea mountain. The sky was a soft silver, and the sun filtered through just enough to paint the crests and curves of the medium rough sea a deep gold. The rest of the undulating water was dark silver. Out of the water behind us came flying fish after flying fish. And above them, more than a hundred feet over the water, flew two skydiving man-o'-war birds.

Scott explained, "Most predatory birds have a very high density of cones throughout the back of their retina. We have cones just in the center part of the retina, which is why things that you look at directly are in perfect focus, but the things you see out of the corner of your eye are fuzzy. Now, the man-o'-war birds can see 180 degrees of detail or more. That's why they can cover such a large area when they're flying.

"And that's why I'm always looking for them. There is nothing in the natural world that can give me so much information as these birds.

When they dive down and start hovering over fish, that's a pretty sure indication that the predator fish we seek are there, too. Those birds locate marlin, sailfish, dolphin, mako sharks, great whites—any fast-moving predator fish that chases prey to the top of the ocean.

"My boat's named for those birds," he added. "The man-o'-war has to catch fish to survive—we have to catch fish to survive.

"Fact is," Scott mentioned, "you can even tell what kind and size of fish the man-o'-war is on by the way it flies. For instance, we use the birds a lot to find schooling dolphin—that's the fish, not the mammal. The little schooling fish move erratically, and a bird that is following them will swoop and move from side to side. The bigger fish will tend to move in a straight, deliberate course. So when you see the birds just swooping and not doubling back or varying too much from a straight-line course, then you can almost be assured they're either on the bigger, solitary dolphin or on a billfish like a sailfish or a marlin."

On our way out to the Hump, Scott told me story after story. But we were interrupted by an excited voice crackling over Scott's VHF radio. It was another charter captain, Skippy Nielsen from the *How About It*.

"Skippy's saying that right there where he is, near shore in ten feet of water, there's an eight-hundred-pound tiger shark," Scott interpreted. "It is a little unusual to find one that size in that close."

"Where exactly are they watching him?"

Scott told me, and my mouth suddenly went dry. I'd been snorkeling in the very same area yesterday.

"A tiger shark that large has a big potbelly," Scott told me. "It'll also have a blunt head, a very large mouth, and triangular teeth. Tigers clamp on a piece of food and shake their heads and just sever whatever they've bitten.

"They're very aggressive, too. That would be a bad shark to encounter in the water.

"Other than the great white, which I've seen at the Hump, there is no shark I would be more afraid of," Scott continued. "A tiger shark like they're talking about is a bona fide man-eater. It could just snap you up like a snack—no problem."

Many fishermen have been thrilled to find a feeding school of dolphin, such as these above. They will strike at almost anything thrown into the water. Dolphins are powerful, leap like rockets, and are delicious.

At the end of a day's fishing, charter boats display some of their best catches where they dock. Any boat would like to boast the lineup at the far right: (left to right) two wahoo, an amberjack, another wahoo, a sailfish, another wahoo, and a blackfin tuna.

Sunsets in the Keys are richly colored, influencing all who see them, sweeping them from one mood to another—from intense passion to soul-deep peace. *Florida Bay.*

Of course, the local color includes places like Abel's Tackle Box (right), a must-stop shop if you need ice, fishing supplies, live or frozen bait, a replica of the barracuda you caught and released, or you just want to soak up some atmosphere. *Windley Key.*

GULF OF MEXICO

The Everglades and the Ten Thousand Islands

The wildest, least inhabited area of the whole Florida Gulf Coast is a seventy-five-mile stretch that, by my reckoning, begins at a place called East Cape, at the southwestern tip of the Everglades, and ends at the fishing community of Goodland, on Marco Island.

Cruising along the coast, I expected to see acres of saw-grass marsh because that was how I envisioned the Everglades. The marsh, however, is inland. What I saw was an irregular collection of mangrove islands, none of which could be inhabited comfortably by people, yet some were home to a few hermit squatters. From above, the islands look

like deep green lace arranged on milky green water. The area is called the Ten Thousand Islands.

For the few Florida natives who draw their living from this area—mainly by net fishing—survival is a daily priority. I met and lived with these rarest of Americans for a couple of months.

They are a stolid, tight-lipped people with an unbelievable will to live in an area so wild as this, an area that once was their home before the federal government made it into the massive Everglades National Park. Slowly they open up to strangers who become friends. People like me.

In 1995 net fishing within three to eight miles of the Florida coast was outlawed. Again, the wild-water people of South Florida will have to adapt to survive as their predecessors have done for generations.

A half-basket of pompano (far left) is the highly prized catch of local fishermen. They seek out these fast-moving, skittish fish because they bring a high price at the market.

Marker 7 Fish House (above) is on the edge of the Ten Thousand Islands. Generations of fishermen have brought their catches to this place to be bought and then sold to outlets around the nation and as far away as Japan—but no more. Recent constraints on net fishing have effectively put thousands of fishermen out of work.

Bob and Barb Stinson (left) manage Marker 7 Fish House. They live on the second floor with their "kids," five parrots and two pit bulls. Red and Janet Parker's little daughter pays close attention.

The Ten Thousand Islands is one of the last remaining water wilderness in the continental United States. Yet some of its people have long adapted to the ways of the wild. The local fishermen can watch how the wind moves the fronds on a palm tree (like the one above) and gauge water conditions on the surrounding bays. This day the wind was from the north, gusting with a punchy energy. Boating would have been far too rough "outside," in the open Gulf, away from the protection of the sheltered bays, passes, salt creeks, and narrow inlets.

For generations Gary Weeks's family has drawn its living, however meager, from the Gulf that surrounds the southwestern Florida coast. They homesteaded and pioneered Marco Island long before the word *tourist* was ever spoken on the island. Gary (left) hauls in his net, this time with nothing but a few hardheads, a scavenging saltwater catfish that will be thrown back.

Aboard his boat, the *Family Tradition,* Gary and his brother-in-law, Earl Moore (below), haul in a net they hoped would be loaded with much-sought-after pompano. There were four. But their labors were not in vain when they looked over a fairly good day's harvest (right) of pompano, a few jackfish, and a few Spanish mackerel.

The Parker brothers, Red and Billy, were two of the most fascinating people I met during my voyage. Half-Seminole Indian, half-Irish American, they had grown up in this area and knew no other life. Billy (far left) is a combat veteran of Vietnam. Since returning from Southeast Asia, he prefers to live in the security of the deep swamp, the open ocean, and the shadows.

As white-booted fishermen, Red and Billy and their families barely subsist in an area that is highly prized by land development companies and environmentalists. Despite their native Floridian heritage, it is becoming more and more difficult for them to make their living from the sea. The two brothers posed by one of the boats (upper left) at Marker 7 Fish House with two of Red's children and Billy's wife, Robin.

To navigate the shallows throughout the Ten Thousand Islands, local fishermen developed a boat with the motor mounted in the middle.

BILLY AND RED PARKER have lived on the water and made their livings from it all their lives. The Parker family, native Floridians, homesteaded in the Everglades. They are a rare breed. What they told me about growing up here and alligator hunting was chilling.

"My family all lived on the islands, mostly in the Ten Thousand Islands, but up in the Fort Myers area, too—around the little town of Fort Myers Beach. We followed the fish, lived on our boat." Billy spoke of these times with a muscular pride. "Dad used to take his skiff and put his poling oar up in the center of the boat and put up a sail, and we'd sail the skiff from one place to the next because we didn't have outboard motors at that time.

"Our Daddy was a strong, fair man," Billy went on. "Rough in his own kind of ways. He was five-eleven, about 180 pounds, broad-shouldered, red hair, fair-complected. Red favors him a lot.

"Daddy grew up fishin', huntin' gators, eatin' curlew, sellin' feathers for hats. We fished with him as soon as we could go in the boat. We did a lot of our travelin' in a sixteen- to seventeen-foot skiff. We would mainly go three or four or five days at a time to catch our fish. Then we'd just salt our fish down and we'd cover them with the mangrove limbs to keep them from spoiling—keep the sun off of them. When we needed extra income, Daddy hunted gators and coons.

"He couldn't afford to have a stainless-steel gun, and a normal one would rust all to pieces. So most of the time we'd hunt the gators with a hatchet. We'd do it right at dark, when they were becoming active. Dad would get in the water just about up to his neck. Dad could make all the sounds a gator could make—bellow, grunt, mating sounds. He knew when the gator was coming 'cause he could see the wake from the gator coming at him. He hit 'em right between the eyes with his hatchet—he knew right when to drop the hatchet into the gator's head.

"After Daddy hit the gator it was supposed to be dead. But I was the one that had to swim out for the alligators and, of course, a lot times they weren't dead. So I've had to wrestle a few alligators in my time as a young boy. I began doing that when I was seven."

An osprey (right) holds a toad fish in its talons on top of Marker 1. Ospreys are gifted at catching fish; they make spectacular dives from high above into the water to snatch their prey.

Handmade of marine-grade plywood (below), this shallow-water boat is called a bird-dog boat. It was once used for net fishing, which is no longer allowed in Florida waters. New uses will have to be devised. *Goodland*.

The crosspiece of a dock's charred remains (far right) supports the delicate legs of seven sandpipers. *Southern Marco Island Bridge*.

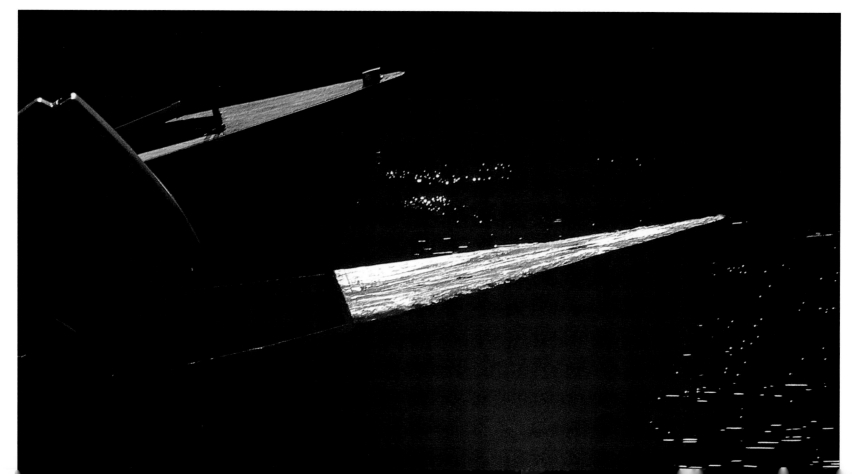

Larry Thompson (left) mends his net after a large shark tore through it. This net is designed to catch small fish the size of mullet, sheepshead, and pompano. *Coon Key Pass.*

A fisherman's hands have to be able to do the delicate work of mending a monofilament net, yet be strong enough to haul in and empty the always-hoped-for-but-seldom-realized full net of marketable fish.

When the South Florida sky begins to fill with fast-moving low gray clouds, the air cools, and even the protected waters begin to have waves, the fishermen quickly return to their home ports. The elements can be brutal to a ship of any size, and the Gulf can be very unforgiving.

A time comes for every boat when its seagoing days are over. Some are beached to either rot or be rebuilt. *Goodland.*

The Jungle Woods

T he woodlands and seldom-seen coastline of Taylor, Dixie, Jefferson, and Wakulla Counties form a region known as the Big Bend of Florida. Like the Ten Thousand Islands and the Dry Tortugas, the Big Bend is another part of this continually amazing country that I had never heard of before this trip.

At times the Big Bend seemed to be as isolated as Alaska. This remote place is part wetland jungle, part scrubland, part prairie, part marsh, and part swamp, all crisscrossed with long fingers of high pine forest. Bubbling up throughout the area are some of the largest springs in the world. So much water comes from the springs, such as Wakulla Springs, that rivers are formed with some of the purest and clearest water in the world.

Black bear still roam here, though mostly unseen. I followed one set of tracks along a beach that was half-covered with derelict tree stumps. Wide-headed bull alligators prey on otters

55

occasionally. In the humid early evenings, black-and-white wood storks nest in the crooked, moss-mangled cypresses. Dinosaur bones lie by the hundreds in the rivers generated by the springs.

These jungle woods offer exotic flora and fauna beauty to anyone willing to venture into an area where the creature comforts are still reserved for the creatures.

In the Wakulla River (left), chilled spring water on an early summer morning generates dense fog around this tree and a lone egret. On the untamed banks of the Aucilla River (above), cattle egrets roost on a dead tree. Before the penetrating Florida sun can burn off the fog on Wakulla Springs (right), a limpkin searches for snails on floating aquatic plants.

These are rare sights around most highly developed Gulf Coast locations, but they are very common in the Big Bend. Their commonplaceness, however, generates a complacency about their preservation. And these are indeed rare places in need of protection.

A limpkin (above) lets the warming morning sunlight dry its damp feathers as it perches on a vibrant cypress tree whose base is more than ten feet around. Apple snail eggs (right) wait to hatch on the bark of this tree and may eventually become a meal for the limpkin. *Wakulla River.*

There are few mature examples of slow-growing cypress trees (left) remaining in the state although they once filled the Florida wetlands. They are rarely, if ever, replanted because of their slow growth rate. *Steinhatchee.*

Bald cypresses are one of the few trees in North America that can grow in water. Their wood does not rot, making it invaluable to the early Gulf Coast settlers for homes, barns, and docks. *Wakulla River.*

The palms rise above the jungle (above) along the banks of the Saint Marks River. When darkness comes, the alligators follow familiar trails through the wild growth and into the river to hunt.

White egret wings (left) gracefully flap through the soft gray fog of the upper Steinhatchee River.

I went around many bends in this river (right) and saw almost no evidence of human habitation. Just beneath the surface of the dark brown water lie boat-sinking limestone boulders, preserving the wildness of the Aucilla River.

D URING THE 1980s, drug smuggling made the Aucilla River one of the most heavily used wild rivers in the country. A person in the Big Bend area told me of his past involvement with the drug trade. At the time, he was a real estate agent. One day a small group of men came to see him.

"They said that they had a guy in South Florida who needed a place to offload shrimp boats and a place to warehouse the cargo. They didn't say the word *pot*. I showed them all these different places.

"Finally it came down to two of the least known, most untouched, most hidden rivers in America, the Econfina and the Aucilla. The Aucilla actually goes underground for several miles and resurfaces later. No more than a handful of people live along the banks of either river. They chose the Aucilla."

One still morning when the air was smooth, I set out on the *Cooper* to explore the mouth of the Aucilla River. Because the bright green marsh extends well beyond the solid ground and creates a kind of vegetative maze, the actual river entrance is hard to find.

For the first mile and a half through the bay and into the mouth of the river, there was marsh everywhere—high grass that took root underwater

and grew like a green field above. Every so often I'd see a piece of high ground where a lone palm tree or salt cedar tree stood.

By the time the Aucilla narrowed into a real river I might have been hundreds of miles up the Amazon. The undulating growth and pressured quiet of this river jungle were overpowering.

The riverbanks were loaded with old stumps and even entire washed-up trees, weathered and gray, stacked like giant bones. On the banks, plant life intertwined in an orgy of vines, tree trunks, and Spanish moss, which hung like a gray veil over everything. I could not see more than a few feet through the tangle of vegetation. The riverbank and surrounding swamp and jungle were a perfect environment for giant diamondback rattlers and the stinking, venomous cottonmouths. Locals said that some were as thick as boa constrictors, terrifying.

A small chameleon, its color a tropical green, floated by me on a golden-tan palm leaf. Alligator gars, prehistoric-looking fish with heads like alligators, rolled on the surface to gulp air, then slyly sunk from sight as soon as they saw me. I could see where gators had been slithering and crawling in and out of the river; the wild marsh grass trampled into narrow trails where they had dragged their heavy bodies. Never have I been on an American river so primeval, a place where plants and animals reigned as if the earth held no humans. Now I understood why the smugglers had chosen the Aucilla.

A second before I took the picture to the far left, this wide-headed bull gator was as still as a black rock atop a mass of aquatic plants. This alligator's coloring is blue-black because it lives in the pure, cool waters of the Wakulla River.

In a quieter moment, I encountered a brown pelican (left) floating atop the dark waters of the Steinhatchee River.

In the Big Bend of Florida (below), this seven-foot alligator warms its chilled blood after a night's hunting in the Wakulla River.

BLOODWORTH'S DRUGSTORE is right across the street from the new Taylor County Courthouse in Perry, Florida. Things don't change much in Taylor County, and they change even less at Bloodworth's. You can get a great egg-and-olive sandwich for $1.35 and an old-fashioned chocolate milkshake mixed in a stainless-steel canister for $1.15. You can also have a borderline otherworldly tour of the place given gleefully by Mr. James Bloodworth, proprietor.

Bloodworth's Drugstore has been a gathering place for decades. The people of Taylor County all seem to love James Bloodworth. Visitors and customers sit on spinning, white metal seats in front of a marble counter that was installed in 1936. They "visit" as they sip their delicious shakes.

The lighting is soft and cooling. In the front of the store is an old weight machine that still tells your weight for a penny. Behind the weight machine is a Kodak sign advertising film. It is practically new—only about ten or fifteen years old. Behind the soda fountain counter hangs a needlepoint slogan given to Mr. Bloodworth by his church: "When ye are in the service of your fellow beings, ye are in the service of your God."

On display for free is Mr. Bloodworth's private bottle collection. There right in front of me was an Aunt Jemima pancake syrup bottle, maybe a year or two old. It was part of the collection. There was a jelly jar from Knott's Berry Farm, maybe a year old. All the bottles were on a pink shelf that ran the length of the store. Underneath was makeup, most of it made by Yardley in the 1960s. The eye shadow is in "mod" shades of pale blue, pale green, and pale purple.

I then spotted something on the shelves that looked really old. It was cough syrup, on sale for seventy-five cents. The label assured me that it did not contain any habit-forming drugs. Mr. Bloodworth said, "Today that would sell for at least four dollars, maybe four-fifty." He said that particular batch of cough syrup had been for sale here maybe fifty years. *Fifty* years!

Most amazing of all was the small cardboard box on the shelf, discolored with age, that announced, "Dr. LeGear's Nerve Sedative Tablets for Dogs, Puppies and Cats." The box held pet tranquilizers dating back to the 1930s and 1940s.

Near the box of pet sedatives was a decongestant called, "666 Cold Preparation." James commented that some local people may have taken the 666 on the label to mean the product was associated with Satan. Maybe that was the reason there were still a couple of boxes for sale after thirty years or more!

The undeveloped banks of the Steinhatchee River are thick with exotic natural beauty, such as this section of limestone rock, twisted salt cedar, palm fronds, and deep green.

The word *retired* takes on a whole new meaning around Denver Fleming of Steinhatchee, Florida. A long-time resident, like almost everyone else, he came to Florida from somewhere else. Denver came from Oregon and worked for many years as a seafood buyer for a large Florida grocery chain on the Atlantic Coast. As that region began to fill, he and his wife looked for a place like the old Florida they had once known. They found it on the Steinhatchee River, just a mile or so from the open Gulf, in the small village of Steinhatchee. From the Ideal Fish Camp, Denver now guides fishermen in search of speckled trout. He has also become an outspoken proponent for protecting the woodlands, the watershed, the wetlands, the marine world, and especially the delicate grass flats of the Big Bend.

At midday, I could look out over the Steinhatchee River and not believe I was in Florida. In many ways, the Big Bend area resembled what I thought the great tropical rain forests of Central and South America might look like.

A group of egrets sits undisturbed on the upper end of the Steinhatchee River.

The Perfect Beaches

Many of my friends familiar with the beaches between Ochlockonee Point, Florida, and Gulf Shores, Alabama, don't want too many people to know just how perfect these beaches are. I understand how they feel about this gorgeous stretch of coastline. Too much development could spoil yet another pristine gift of nature. The problem is in knowing how much growth is too much.

There is no way, however, that the secret can be kept. Yet the more we know about the dunes and beaches around Gulf Shores or near Saint Joseph Peninsula, the more we realize how rare and precious is Grayton Beach or Top Sail Beach or Saint Andrews Beach, and the greater the steps we can take to protect them. They stand as precious as a Picasso and as enjoyable as the best music.

Sand and water, dunes and beaches like these are incredible gifts to the world that lift us up and cleanse our souls. Everyone needs to know of them, and everyone needs to protect them.

When I anchored in the shallow waters off this beach and walked ashore, the time could have been 1791 or 1891 rather than 1991. This is the primeval way almost all beaches looked before anyone "owned" them. One hundred feet from here, I found fresh black bear tracks. *Ochlockonee Point, east of Apalachicola.*

To see these massive dunes on either side of Florida Highway 87 from a car window or from a speeding boat, it is easy to overlook the specks of yellow wildflowers. I stopped and wandered among them and found, not only the whitest sand, but here and there delicate wildflowers growing low and brilliantly. The battering winds keep them low, but the bright white sand frames them so their colors show vibrantly. *Santa Rosa Island, south of Pensacola.*

Laughing gulls (left) await the night on a tree trunk that has drifted onto the beach. *Ochlockonee Point.*

Like many beach lovers, I like to roam the beach, timing myself so I will arrive back at the beach house, my boat, or wherever I'm staying in time for the sunset. At that moment, the colors of the sky and land and water are deep and dense and luscious. And the bugs are not yet out. *Alligator Point, south of Tallahassee.*

Docks come in many shapes and conditions. They can be elaborate or primitive, just a couple of crude logs jammed into the mud and topped with some warped and rotting pieces of decking, but they all lead to something important. A dock can lead to your boat or to crab traps or to the place where you store your windsurfer or wave runner. It can be the place where you watch the moon illuminate the waters you know and love.

I RECEIVED a short lesson in geology from Dr. Bill Tanner of Florida State University. When I commented on the whiteness of the sand on the beaches in North Florida and South Alabama, he explained that most beach sand comes from the erosion of the continents.

If you have a large coral reef, as we do in extreme southern Florida in the Keys, then most of the beaches are made up of coral and seashell debris. In other areas, almost all the sand comes from the hills. Rivers and glaciers have been grinding the material until it's carried to the coast and is distributed by tidal action along the shore.

Sand receives its color from organic or mineral mixtures. Reddish sand contains iron oxide. Grayer sand contains an organic material that either coats the sand grains or is intermingled. What we think of as pure sand is quartz, which is chemically similar to glass. Pure sand is as clear as glass, but when it's piled up on the beaches and dunes, the overall appearance is white because of the way the quartz reflects refracted light.

The sand along the west coast of Florida is white because it has been reworked repeatedly by the tidal motion of the Gulf. The waves may not be all that energetic, but they don't have to be all that big if they get a good crack at the sand.

Apparently, most of the barrier islands were formed during a small drop in sea level. Sea level fluctuates three to six feet every couple of centuries. Should it drop six feet in an area where a sandbar has been accumulating, an island emerges. Two things can happen. If the wave energy is high and the sand on the island is limited, the island will erode into nothing. If the wave energy is low and there is plenty of sand, the island may even grow.

The perfect beaches are not limited to the area between Ochlockonee Point and Gulf Shores. I found an extraordinary beach (above) on Useppa Island.

Ospreys (right) rest on the chimney of a beach home on Useppa Island.

Being on an island, on a beach, gives me a chance to relax, to revert to a childlike state of joy that lets me want to sit in a tree swing like this one and rock and enjoy the moment. At times like this I can hear the moss swaying in the hot afternoon air. I smell the camellia blooms. Life is perfect for some minutes, some hours, some days. A lone light (right) marks the entrance to a crooked sand path through a grove of bamboo and pines to a cabin by the bay. *Useppa Island.*

The wind doesn't know it creates art like this (far left). This blue-white sand dune is the canvas for these delicate wavy lines, accentuated by wisps of grass. *Grayton Beach.*

Details are very important to me, the small pieces of our earth. It is here I find much inspiration, the delicate nuances of existence, as I found in these flowers with bird tracks gently imprinted on the soft sand that had been shaped by a wind coming from the north. *Gulf Shores, Alabama.*

83

Like all children growing up on the coast, you
have to dip your toes into the huge, scary ocean
that seems to stretch all the way to God. As
children become more comfortable with the
water, they submerge their feet—wading,
swimming, exploring the shallows. Here (above)
the Rice brothers, Alex and Jesse, net and pails in
hand, search for horseshoe crabs, slow-moving
minnows, whatever they can catch. As they grow
older, if they stay on the coast, the boys will
probably go farther out to sea.

All along the Gulf, families come back year after
year to summer homes like this one (right) where
many memories live.

Wilcox County, Alabama

Many rivers empty into the Gulf of Mexico, forming two-way corridors between the coast and the interior of the continent. Settlement along these river ways was influenced by the fertility of the surrounding land and the access the water provided to larger ports. This is how Wilcox County attracted its population in the early 1800s.

I journeyed up the Alabama River more than two hundred miles to find this world of undiluted southernness. I'd never been anywhere where the present is so blended with the past. In this world, *you* is strongly connected to *your family,* and your family extends back as far as memory allows. Here, family land and original homes are rarely sold, usually passed down.

Stories from 130 years ago are told today as if they had happened only yesterday. I was riding through downtown Camden, the county seat, when the southern gentlewoman next to me pointed to a man, saying, "That is a carpetbagger." The man was a descendant of a northerner who had come to the region 125 years ago, following the Civil War. His relatives had purchased some land from my friend's family, land that they had to sell to pay taxes at a time when most southerners had no money.

Prior to the Civil War the Alabama River was loud and busy with steam-powered paddle wheelers. Almost all freight was brought up from Mobile and all cash crops, especially cotton, were shipped there. When the fall harvest had ended, many planters trekked to the great city via the river for the city's Mardi gras.

Cotton was king in Wilcox County, prior to the War Between the States. Now it's not even a prince. Today pine trees are king, but they cannot provide the landowners with enough income to let them live in the manner their ancestors once knew. Today's income also comes from cattle and hunting leases.

Not far off Highway 21, atop a small hill, stands this once lively home built during the antebellum period, which is fortunately being restored. *Furman*.

These Wilcox County ladies (left) have played bridge together for almost fifty years, sharing each other's rewards, tragedies, and every days. They are, from left to right, Scottie Goodbold, Virginia Cook (seated), Mabel Lane, Hattie Riggs (seated), and Laure Johnson. *Cooks Hill.*

The card game is not so important now for these ladies as when they met. Family history has taken on more importance. Some in the bridge club can trace their family lines back to the Magna Carta. Some belonged to the Magna Carta Dames and also to the Daughters of the American Revolution. Probably the one organization that makes them feel strongest about their place in the world is the United Daughters of the Confederacy. To become a member, these women had to prove they were descended from a man who fought for the South during the War Between the States.

One of the members of the club wrote the following essay on "Why I Am a Daughter of the Confederacy":

I am a daughter of the Confederacy because I was born a daughter of the Confederacy. A part of my heritage was that I came into this world with the blood of a soldier in my veins. A soldier who may have had nothing more to leave behind to me and to those who come after me, except the heritage. A heritage so rich in honor and glory that it far surpasses any material wealth that could be mine. But it is mine to cherish, to nurture, and to pass along to those yet to come. I am therefore a daughter of the Confederacy because it is my birthright. I am a daughter of the Confederacy because I can no more help being a daughter of the Confederacy than I can help being an American, and I feel I was greatly favored by inheriting a birthright from both.

This decorative gingerbread on the porch pillar was not added to hold up this porch's roof but to excite the eye. *Camden*.

During the antebellum period, this home on a high hill not far from the Alabama River was built by the Cook family. Today, all these years later, the hill is still known as Cooks Hill. Most of the descendants are buried in the precisely tended family cemetery, just a hundred yards to the side of the house.

In many places in the South, old barns and old homes hold cherished memories. As opposed to being bulldozed, they are allowed to stand and lean. Sometimes, out of respect for the memories, they are allowed to slowly collapse if there is no money to save them.

Before washing machines, most laundry in the South was done in pots like the one to the right. The water was heated by wood fires, and the clothes were washed with lye soap.

Marian Furman, standing with her mother, Minnie Leah Purdue, comes from one of the oldest families in Wilcox County. Her family tree features a 1930s Alabama governor; an exotic, cheese-loving, crossword-puzzle-expert, never-married uncle; a ranching and farming matriarch called Mama Clyde; and many other potent characters.

Marian is the county photographer. Her husband, Herb, is the local surveyor. The Furmans have ten children from age twenty to thirty-four. I lived with the Furmans for several months in their large, white house, having first been invited for just one night. It was so fine to be part of a family again.

Marian has a smile that lights up her deep brown eyes. Since her children and her husband and her mother give her plenty to smile about, she is almost always happy.

The paint may fade, the money may be gone, and the people sired by the builders of these once grand southern homes may have moved to Chicago or Atlanta or New York, but the pride of family accomplishment only grows stronger. These homes are shrines to southern blood, often kept even if only marginally maintained.

The columns and the front porch (right), the proud face of this old home, are the last to fade to gray.

Everywhere you look, the barns and sheds are covered with tin roofs. The sun and the rain have painted each panel individually. *Cooks Hill.*

EVERY ONCE in a while, I develop a crush on someone I meet on my journeys. Minnie Leah Purdue, here next to me, is one. Her daughter, Marian Furman, took this picture for me. The Furmans were my family for a short while.

Minnie Leah is frail now in body; she told me she always has had a delicate system. But in her youth, during the Roaring Twenties, she had been a vibrant though delicate flower, and people say she danced with an effortless, heavenly grace. Minnie Leah has kept all her dance cards from all the parties of her youth. I loved the massaging, sweet tones of her voice, which was slightly above a whisper. Every word was spoken with precision.

"Daddy farmed. He had sharecroppers, and he was a better judge than he was a farmer. I can say that about him. He enjoyed the farm, but he didn't get too much money out of it. We had a good many black people living on the place, and then at his death, my mother carried on. She was really a better farmer than my father ever was.

"We were all Democrats; almost all southern people were then. *Republican* at that time was an ugly word. One time my father told my mother, he says, 'Clyde, look, you see that man over there?' Mama says yes. 'Well, he's a Republican.' And I looked to see what a Republican would look like.

"A lot of people had the attitude about Mama like they did about Roosevelt—that she would save us all. If any white person ever mistreated any one of the black people who lived on our place, she would go and storm at that person, warn him never to do that, never again. She just treated everyone fairly, and they could depend on her. If someone needed to go to the doctor or the hospital, she would take them and pay for it.

"Mama was one of two ladies who went to Europe with the Associated Women Farmers of America. She was an adventuresome woman.

"On their way to Europe in a big ship, crossing the Atlantic, a storm came up one night. All the ladies were scared to death, crying and praying. You know what Mama did? She went and put on a very expensive handmade blouse, said if she was going down on that ship, she was going down looking pretty. She brought that blouse home, and I still have it." Minnie Leah cherishes memories. She is the keeper of many of them for this family.

"Our family came here from South Carolina on both my mother's side and my father's side. They were coming from South Carolina to Alabama, and they were going through Indian territory, and the father got very ill, so the wife bedded him down in the back of the wagon. She put on his clothes and put her hair up under her cap. Then she drove the wagon through Indian territory, pretending she was a man. And she made it. So that's one of our ancestors.

"We all have a little saying we use real often: Just keep on driving the wagon. Because that's what our ancestor did, and that's what we've all had to do."

In the earliest days of the South, roads were made by scraping out a single lane with mule-drawn metal blades. Very few such roads remain. *Snow Hill.*

Sally Mae Ramsey lives alone now. She heats with wood and keeps in touch with her friends by phone, as none of them gets around much anymore. *Whiskey Run Road.*

A church steeple (right) points to heaven even though some siding is lacking on the portion that doesn't face the road. When not in use, an incredible stillness settles around the tiny country church (far right). Yet on Sunday the joy and energy and shouting and singing will be uninhibited, filling the woods and spilling out into the road. *Snow Hill.*

A sharecropper's shack gradually loses the battle with gravity. After slavery had been abolished, sharecropping became the usual procedure for farming a landowner's often thousand-acre-plus tract of land. Today, no sharecroppers live or work the Hollinger place; the work is done by tractors, the owners, and a few hired men.

Venturing closer to the collapsing shack, I found the walls covered with the remnants of old newspapers. The sharecroppers used the newspaper as insulation and a weather barrier to keep the cold winter wind out. Thus the walls of many tenant homes came to be "papered" with white faces.

Is there any more stereotypical picture of a summer's day in the Deep South? This hound finds comfort in his owner's Chevy pickup, enjoying the occasional shade and the coolness of the metal truck bed. Dog days are every day in the country.

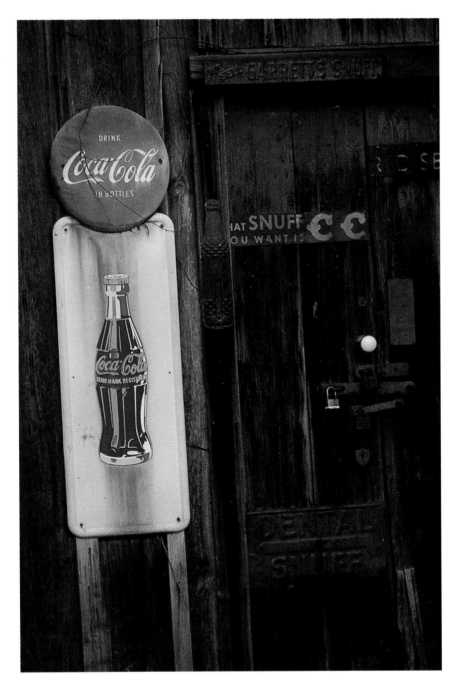

Not too long ago, each plantation had its own dry goods store. This tiny store (right), its doors long closed, still advertises Coca-Cola, popular in little green bottles in the 1940s.

Country stores in Alabama and throughout the South did more than sell food and drinks. They were also social centers for the community. News like who was sick, who was having financial difficulty, that Dorothy had twins, that Thomas caught a twenty-five-pound catfish was spread by word of mouth. Store owners became town criers as they talked with their customers when the time came to tally a purchase. *Coy, Alabama.*

Daisy Durante (left) brought me to her old home. As she described the little fence that had surrounded the house at one time, she also pointed out where she had once planted and nurtured some roses—red, pink, and white—and lilies.

Almost all southern families have built lifelong relationships between whites and African Americans. Pictured to the lower left are Marian Furman (center, back); two of her daughters, Laura (left) and Teresa (right); and Carrie Williams (seated). Carrie worked for Marian's grandmother, Mama Clyde, for fifteen years. Because of that time together, these women are linked for life.

There are fourteen elected officials in Wilcox County, and twelve are African Americans. The central issue in any election has proven to be character, not color. Janet Knight works for the county before returning to college to work toward her master's degree. She stands at the courthouse's west entrance, near a plaque commemorating a family's contribution to the Southern cause in the Civil War.

AT AGE SIXTEEN, Daisy married Rob Durante, a very dark and handsome man from Wilcox County who had been working on a bridge-building crew in Conecuh County. He'd seen Daisy standing in the yard.

The young couple first sharecropped on a plantation near Pineapple. There was then, as there is now, an underground of information about who were the best people to work for, who would actually give you your fair share. Marian Furman's grandmother, Mama Clyde, was one of these—some say the best. Many black sharecroppers wanted to come and live on her place, rent some of her land, and farm. Daisy and Rob moved to a house on one of Mama Clyde's farms, not far down from Whiskey Run, a road where a lot of land-owning blacks have always lived.

"I loved our place there," Daisy said to me so many times. They settled there in the early 1930s, during the Great Depression.

"Rob," Daisy said, "was a good farmer. He wanted to work all his life in the fields. But I was working for white peoples, too. I kept white people in my mind."

Daisy and Rob lived in a little wood-frame house for almost sixty years. When I met her, it had been about two years since Daisy reluctantly moved from that house near the narrow creek. She left only after Rob had suffered a couple of devastating heart attacks and finally had to be placed in the nursing home. Daisy couldn't look after the place by herself. But she missed it terribly, and she didn't like living in town.

She'd asked me if I would take her out to her house, and of course I did. I knew how much someone could miss their land, their place on earth.

"We had a cute little fence around the house, sure did. That's when I had my pretty flowers, had red roses and pink roses and white roses and big old lilies. I used to carry them to Mama Clyde all the time to set on the dinner table when they had company.

"I just enjoyed it so much down here. I love it. And I like to farm. I sure do. I'm a girl belong right out here in the country." Daisy

held her cane like a feather. She stepped lightly. Her soft ebony eyes glowed with remembrance.

She pointed behind the house, recalling when everything was so neat, so groomed, so cared for. Now dried ragweed grew a few feet up the faded blue siding. "We used to have a corncrib there. It was a big old crib, and we'd load it up with corn. We had a nice pecan tree right there. Sure did.

"Oh, that house was so cute. I had it fixed up so nice then. It had a cute little wood stove, and I loved it, too. We had a pump—we got our water out of the well. I loved to go pump water. I'd pump the water every evening right over there.

"Oh, that water was so pretty and good. That's the only kind of water we used. We took baths in a tin tub in the kitchen. I'd put a dishpan of water on the stove. Rob's water was on the stove to take his bath first. Then I'd put the children's dishpan of water and give them their baths, and then I'd put my dishpan of water and take my bath. That water felt so nice and warm. Sure did.

"Then we had a chicken yard over there, and a hog pen down there, and the milk cows over there. We grew everything. Peas, beans, peppers, eggplant, just everything. Butter beans, okra—we just had everything—corn, beets, watermelon, and cantaloupes. I'd plant everything I saw in the catalogs, even that bean that looks like a rattlesnake!

"Didn't have to worry about anything. Got ready to cook anything, we could do it. We had a smokehouse right in the back out there where we smoked our meat and our sausage. We had our living. Had everything. I just enjoyed it so much here."

Not far from the high banks of the Alabama River, a well-kept Liberty Hill still lives (right), although some shutters are drawn.

Are there times when southerners long for the days past? Gerry Burford (far right) stands on the porch of a house that was once the center of a large plantation. During heritage days, tours of historic homes are given by the ladies of the community who dress up as it used to be and serve as guides to the old homes. Wilcox County has the second most antebellum homes in Alabama.

One of the first homes in Camden (far left) houses no one now as wisteria vines almost cover it. At one time the abandoned rocking chair (left) was an integral element of the porch behind, which has now rotted away. While the family is gone from this home (above), these portraits of generations past remain as a testimony to the lives that gave this house a life of its own so long and such a short time ago.

GULF OF MEXICO

Along the Mississippi River

Some of the most astounding, most outrageous people and places in America are along the lower Mississippi River. This is true, not only of New Orleans, but in places I'd never known before, such as Yscloskey, Louisiana. I found this to be true also at Southwest Pass, one of the mouths of the river. I found it also in Pilottown, Buras, and Empire. I was amazed at the Croatian-American oystering community that began in Barataria Bay in houses on stilts on the water.

Of course, when it comes to food, there's no better place to eat than New Orleans. The emphasis here is much more on food than on the surroundings, and my new favorite restaurant is an example: Uglesich's. Oysters and seafood have no better venue to my taste.

Ship traffic is unique on the Delta and around New Orleans. World-roaming ships, some more than several hundred feet long and worth more than fifty million dollars, traverse this great river way, making it one of the most used commercial waterways in the world.

The people who live here make this place unforgettable. They work hard, but they also play hard, dance without stopping, and eat well every day. They let the good times and the bad times roll and handle them all with grace and ease. They refuse to be like everyone else and define themselves stunningly in the process.

The unusual is the norm in New Orleans (pronounced Noo Awlins). Jazz and Dixieland music in the streets happen every day. Few feet stay still to that background and those rhythms. Everyone eats like every day is a holiday. Boredom, the same old same old. What's that? The restraint and reined-in living characteristic of the heartland is not to be found in New Orleans.

Jackson Square, a block off the Mississippi River, is like a one-hundred-ring circus. Acrobats, preachers, painters, poets, musicians, stand-up comics, schemers, people combing the hair on their legs all perform for tips or for free. Above left, a card reader promises to offer something insightful to an inquiring customer. Even the mules are dressed on the wild side.

Hundreds of entertainers perform for tips on the streets of the French Quarter. A beaded mime (far left), Gorilla Woman (above), and a mustachioed one-man band (left) make any visit to Royal Street unforgettable.

Uglesich's has little to offer diners in the way of slick surroundings, but this is the place to come if you want to eat some of the best shrimp, oysters, crab, and speckled trout on the planet. The restaurant at 1238 Baronne Street is open only for lunch, but that's the best meal of the day for everyone who eats here. George Fisher (right) was a delivery man for thirty years, bringing French bread to Uglesich's for all that time. Now retired, he still delivers, not bread, but entertainment. George comes in every so often and belts out Tom Jones and Frank Sinatra numbers. The diners' reactions range from delighted to slightly bewildered.

My Cajun friends George Dantin and Leon Audibert (below) show off some excellent speckled trout we caught one night with our boat tied up to an offshore oil rig. The rig's lights attract shrimp and minnows that are bite-size snacks for these trout. We also caught all the red fish and black drum we wanted. Our arms ached we caught so many fish, a rare thing even for the excellent fishing around the Louisiana coast. *Shell Beach*.

A versatile bay boat docked after a busy day around Shell Beach.

Our fishing poles took a brief rest for the night. George and I had spent the day on the Gulf, and we were going to spend the night at the mouth of the Mississippi River. We had made the short trip into the open Gulf to some offshore oil rigs and caught some red snapper. George used one to make a Cajun fish stew. *Southwest Pass.*

The wild edge of a dark, still-water Louisiana bayou (above). *West of Yscloskey.*

South of New Orleans, on the west bank of the Mississippi, these egrets (left) gathered together, preening before their nighttime rest. *Between Port Sulphur and Myrtle Grove.*

Two Croatian oystermen (left) pose on their cousin's boat after sorting a haul of oysters from Barataria Bay. Croatians originally settled around the southernmost reaches of the Mississippi River. With names like Petrovich, Cvitanovich, and Uglesich, they made their homes around Buras, Empire, and Venice. An oysterboat (above), home-ported in Empire, puts out its nets during shrimping season.

In Louisiana, oystermen own underwater leases, tracts of ocean bottom where only they can harvest oysters. The boundaries are marked with tall, slender bamboo limbs (far right). Seed oysters are planted so they will attach to large oyster shells.

For oyster connoisseurs, there is nothing better than an oyster only minutes after being dredged from the bay (upper right).

T HE LUNCH RUSH was over. A huge man, each arm as big as an oar and covered in dark hair, his body filling up the door frame, toted in a burlap sack. He was the oysterman, Dave Cvitanovich. The burlap sacks he delivered were filled with perfectly plump oysters, the very best, dredged from down below New Orleans in bays settled by Yugoslavians.

Early in the century, many Yugoslavians leaped into the Mississippi River from their country's cargo ships and swam ashore to become Americans. Some built small wooden homes on stilts in Bastian Bay and other shallow bays downriver from New Orleans, near the mouth of the Mississippi. Eventually they built a Yugoslav community. At first they were called Tacos. They kept to themselves, spoke their own language, cooked with olive oil and garlic, and worked and worked the waters of the oyster-rich bays.

On either side of the banks of the Mississippi River, far below New Orleans, are a number of shallow bays that have been harvested and replanted with oysters. Most of the time these bays receive the ideal amount of freshwater from the river and just the right amount of saltwater from the Gulf to grow some of the plumpest, tastiest oysters in the world. And it was on these bays that the Yugoslav settlers built their communities and the oyster trade that would make them prosperous in the New World.

Dave ordered a plate of barbecued oysters and new potatoes. I was stuffed with trout, but my mouth still watered at the sight and memory of those oysters. They were easily the best oysters I had ever tasted.

In southern Louisiana (above left), most people are buried above ground. Flooding occurs regularly. When this place is flooded, the caskets often pop out of the crypts and have to be rounded up by boat.

There have to be stories behind an abandoned boat left to disappear into the marsh (above right), but there's no one around to tell them. *Pilottown*.

The blues and whites of the morning create a stark contrast here (far right), slightly beyond the mouth of the Mississippi River, with bright white pelicans in the foreground and a white shrimp boat in the background. Sometimes being on the open sea can be maddening or boring. Sometimes you fear for your life. Sometimes, like this morning, it's like being in another world.

A shrimp net (left) is pulled up, about to be dumped and sorted on deck. Shrimp will be placed in one pile, edible blue crabs in another, and a few softshell crabs will make another. A typical haul will also include a couple of good-sized flounders, and some small fish and crabs. Those that are still alive will be thrown back, but a lot will have died while in the net.

Nets spread out like wings (above) are set to capture shrimp. Often the fishermen will find little or nothing, other times they will find some shrimp, but rarely will they haul in the always-hoped-for mother lode.

Cargo ships from everywhere come to the Mississippi River, heading for the Port of New Orleans or the hundreds of other ports of call. This Italian freighter, its business done for now, passes the dock at Pilottown. Having come more than a hundred miles from New Orleans, the ship is almost to the open Gulf.

Massive ships enter the mouth of the Mississippi River here at the beginning of Southwest Pass. They move twenty-four hours a day. While a ship is a mile or so out in the Gulf, a pilot is brought aboard to assume the helm from the captain. The pilot captains the ship a short way to Head of the Passes, beyond which is Pilottown, where a river pilot comes aboard and captains the ship to New Orleans.

CAPTAIN ALVIN KLINE, a member of the Crescent River Pilots Association, seemed to enjoy explaining his work to me. I rode with him and other river pilots on the ships they guided up and down the Mississippi River.

"See, a lot of people think when the river is high, it's easier to get a ship up and down the river. But that's not what happens. When the river is high like it is now, it's bringing down a lot of silt. It's muddy, and it's real, real thick because of the silt. As the silt runs downriver, it drops off. You have spots where the current is strong, and you get eddies. The silt just falls to the bottom and builds sandbars at points in the curves of the river, at the mouth of the river, and at the mouth of the Delta. The channels coming up this river change daily. That's where the need for pilots arose.

"The pilot is an adviser to the master of the vessel. He's the local guy who has the knowledge of this river. The first established pilots on the Mississippi were at the mouth in 1722.

"Back then the pilots were rowed out into the river to check and plot the sandbars. With so much sediment washing down the river, the sandbars changed from day to day."

I was with him at the helm of a 732-foot-long Italian freighter as Captain Kline was avoiding a shallow point at milepost 82, going toward the Delta.

"We're staying this far to the left because that point over there is shallow. We've got to be well out in the river because there is a shoal or flat next to it. We're running in eighty-five to ninety feet of water now, and yet three hundred to four hundred feet away from the bank over there the water is only thirty-five feet deep. We need thirty-seven feet. This is a ninety-something-ton ship. Plus as we make this turn, the current will try to push us against the shallows.

"River pilots have to know just how far they need to be from each bank at each point of the river. That's why we pilots are needed to bring these ships up and down the Mississippi."

Smuggling goes on as it has for hundreds of years. The illicit traffic utilizes all kinds of boats: small ones, medium-sized steel-hulled shrimp boats, and even several-hundred-foot-long container tankers. When a boat like the one above, loaded with illegal drugs, grounds on a mud flat or catches fire, there is no call for help. The crew can only hope for a lifeboat and a way ashore.

Cameron Parish, Louisiana

There's a mural about a mile down the road from the Cameron Parish Courthouse. It speaks for the city of Cameron and for the whole parish as well. On one side is a leaping tarpon, on the other a jumping largemouth bass. In between is the statement: Welcome to Cameron—no pollution, no traffic light, no big city life, no city police, no trains, just boats.

The mural also lists the event and the sights for the out-of-towner: the Louisiana Fur and Wildlife Festival, the southwest Louisiana deep sea and inland fishing rodeo, fish, ducks, alligators, muskrats, nutria, birds, shrimp, deer, and twenty-five hundred public-spirited citizens. It ends with a warning: Don't blink twice or you'll miss the time of your life!

Cameron Parish is a lot like the way Louisiana was a long time ago. The people haven't

137

displaced nature; they've tried to share it. For one of the best times of your traveling life, here you'll find miles and miles of marshland, thousands of rare and common water birds, and enchanting narrow ridges that run through the swamp where pure Cajun people live.

Life is everywhere in the marshes and waters of southern Louisiana, though frequently it is hiding, such as this young gull (above) in the marsh grass of Rabbit Island. *The west cove of Calcasieu Lake.*

Thousands of laughing gulls share a rookery island (right)—one of the least seen and most productive in America—with American egrets, roseate spoonbills, and other water birds. *Rabbit Island.*

If they hunker down (far right), all that most people would see is hundreds of snaking snow-white necks and bright yellow beaks growing out of the deep green marsh grass. Born earlier in the year, these common egrets are staying close to home in the protected isolation of Rabbit Island.

Debbie Therriot and the Cameron Parish sheriff everyone calls "Suno," stand in front of the parish courthouse.

DEBBIE THERRIOT was eighteen years old in 1957 when Hurricane Audrey came within a minute of wiping her, her husband, and her parents off the earth. People only had minutes to determine how they would try to survive. A dullness came over her usually sparkling Cajun eyes when she told me about the experience.

"We never worried about storms until Hurricane Audrey hit here. And since then, it's been watch out for the storms and run from the storms when they come in.

"In Little Chenier we had twenty foot of water, and it all came at one time, on a big wave. In that wave were houses, drowned people, animals, snakes, fish, trees, everything. It hit here about seven in the morning.

"Some of the Creole houses that rode that wave got caught right there on the high side of our one-and-only road that dead ends on Little Chenier, where our house was. Me, my mama, daddy, and granddaddy, and our kids all grew up there.

"Then all of a sudden, when that biggest wave came over the road, our house fell apart. We ran and got into one of our marsh boats. We were lucky. We stored all the boats in a boathouse right behind our house. We had only a couple of minutes to do something. All four of us got into a boat, but we couldn't get it started. So we just tied it onto the boathouse until the boathouse blew away, and then we just rode the waves all day in that boat.

"Well, our boat was just a little flatboat about eighteen or twenty feet long and about three feet wide. Jerry and I and my parents were in that boat all day. Actually, we were in and out of the boat. You know, we'd get blown or thrown out, but then we'd catch ahold of the boat and get back in. I don't know how we survived, but it was just like fighting for your life for the next twelve hours, because we were rescued about seven that night.

"The winds were real strong. They would pick up the whole boat. At times we were airborne because the winds were so strong.

"Sometimes we could see around us, sometimes we couldn't. You'd see people you knew all your life blowing by you on some board, a piece of tree. One time we saw a horse standing on top of the side of a barn, surfing by, literally standing atop that wood. All the animals, everything still alive, were trying to find something to crawl on, and they'd crawl into the side of our boat and turn our boat over. We were turned over a whole bunch of times. But we always managed, the four of us, to get back in the boat. Most of the time, I was tied to the boat or tied to Jerry because I was so tiny at that time that the wind would lift me up and try to take me with it.

"Finally after twelve hours we ended up in the Intracoastal Canal, which was about twelve miles through the marsh from our house. We saw a tugboat anchored there, waiting out the storm. They took us aboard."

For Debbie, however, the memories also bring to mind the people she lost to the storm: her godmother and her two children and one particular friend. Her friend's body was never recovered, and Debbie has dreamed the same dream about her for more than thirty-five years. In her dream, her friend has amnesia. Debbie finds her and runs to her, and she hugs her and hugs her.

Some of the best wildlife viewing in America can be done in Cameron Parish, Louisiana, early in the morning as the marsh and swampland come to life or late in the afternoon as the sky moves toward black. Rare water birds, some with bright pink feathers. Alligators as long as a car. Cottonmouths lying where water was moments before, the mud drying on their black skin. Nutria paddling through. Dragonflies with Day-Glo wings. *East of Cameron, off Highway 82.*

A Forster's tern (right) alights gracefully atop a pole near Lower Mud Lake.

The Gulf beaches are used by everyone: families, lovers, smugglers, shell-seekers, fishermen, spring breakers, hermits, and even cows.

A black-gray storm front like this one gives relief from the wilting, all-encompassing heat and humidity if its stiff winds and cold air don't pass directly overhead. Gulf storms, however, often give as much grief as they do relief.

Near Mesquite Ridge (left), three roseate spoonbills, a great blue heron, and a sandpiper work the shallows. A mature roseate spoonbill lands (above). Rare in the United States and found in South Florida and parts of South Louisiana and Texas, they are up to twenty-eight inches tall and have wingspans of fifty-three inches. With their flat spoon-shaped bill, they sift through the shallows and marsh bottoms for food.

Juvenile roseate spoonbills waded away from me as I made my way through the deep marsh grass of Rabbit Island.

There is not much high ground south of Interstate 10 in South Louisiana. The trees are laden with Spanish moss on Little Chenier.

Alligators move with such ease in the warm waters of America, knowing they own it. This one spotted me near Joseph Harbor Bayou.

Sandpipers casually stroll in some shallow water near Crab Lake.

Texas Coastal Cattle Country

A narrow, sandy peninsula juts into Galveston Bay, east of Houston, the largest city in Texas. This sand land couldn't be more different from the city across the bay. The area is blasted by pressure-cooker humidity and scoured by unpredictable hurricanes, making it tough even for cattle and fire ants.

The heat and humidity here have maddened some of the cows and bulls that roam this place, requiring cowboys and horses as rough and tough as they are mean. At least that's what I found at the Whitehead ranch off Highway 562, a couple of miles from Smith Point, Texas.

A pair of calves stand at the edge of the Whitehead herd, off Highway 562, in Chambers County. These are bred to withstand the heat.

Texas cowboys Ronnie Johnson and Ralph Holmes hold back a bunch of cattle too wild to work on foot. Ralph (right) will try to control the wild ones with a whip.

Many coastal Texas ranchers still work cattle together, being neighborly. Because of the constant threat of hurricanes, ranch buildings are constructed knowing that they will be flattened eventually. Alfonso Robles of the Whitehead ranch and Lionel Humphrey, a neighbor from across the road, push these overheated cows and calves into the working chutes.

The corrals at the Whitehead ranch were state of the art. Joe's squeeze chutes were capable of holding the most rambunctious stock.

THERE USED TO BE plenty of tough-as-leather cowboys in the Texas coastal cattle country. There weren't many left by the time I visited. This rarity was why Ralph Holmes, at age seventy-two, cowboyed for two ranches. He worked a lot for Joe Whitehead.

Ralph had been a professional cowboy since he was twelve years old—and there are few anywhere in the world who could claim that they had been cowboying for sixty years. That's cowboying on a working ranch, not show-biz rodeoing. Ralph, who was once a champion rodeo calf roper, knows the difference well.

The first time I saw Ralph was from behind. He was walking toward a truck, leading his slim-built, white-faced horse. And I could see that the space between Ralph's legs had been permanently formed in the exact shape of a horse's midsection, like a Chinese woman's foot that has been bound to become small.

Ralph's leather chaps had been etched by thorns that slap and gouge; he wore them because he had to. His hat had deep, saturated stains from hundreds of unforgiving roundups. Ralph wore gold-rim glasses now. His gray moustache was carefully trimmed. His arms didn't swing. He kept them poised at his side, always ready to yank back on the reins, reach for his rope, pull his hat down harder in the wind, or brace for a charging cow.

Ralph stepped strong, yet his boots did not move fast. In this dead-on summer heat, nothing moved fast unless it thought it was running for its life.

"Yes, sir, whenever they need me I'm here," Ralph said when we had a moment to talk by a clump of tallow trees. "Anymore though, I just work horseback. I don't wrestle the calves now, but I can do the branding and such. My old legs and my knees are getting bad; I can't do a lot of work walking anymore. But on horseback . . . when I'm horseback I can give a man a pretty good day's work.

"Ever since I was six years old and started going to school, I've been riding a horse. You either walked or rode a horse to school. My own first horse, the one that I raised when I was a kid, I called her Pearl. She was a mare. And after I got grown, my favorite roping horse was a big sorrel horse I bought from one of the Jackson brothers. His name was Dude. He was so tall, you could have trouble getting on him. But once you got on him, you were horseback."

Some cattle would just as soon attack you as run from you. Some, like these belonging to Joe and Annette Whitehead, are gentle and calm. Their behavior is based on breeding and the manner in which they're handled.

Ralph's horse, Bald, wants to get after a stray, but his rider holds him back. In summer, everything overheats in the incredibly humid coastal ranching country of Texas. It's so oppressive only the toughest cattle, horses, and people survive. Even then, smart and seasoned Texans work as early in the morning as they can. *Near East Bay, Chambers County.*

Rustling still occurs in this part of Texas, with the stolen cattle often moved to Louisiana. Lionel Humphrey's brand, UN, is done with a running brand (a branding iron with just one short, straight end), one line at a time.

The ranchers try to control their cattle by building very narrow chutes. Nevertheless, one of Lionel's wildest cows tries to leap the fence of an almost inescapable pen. Some cattle seemed as wild as African water buffalo, especially after they started to roar.

Ralph Holmes waits for a couple of high-headed, snorting, roaring, overheated cows to settle down. When they get as out of sorts as they were at this working session, the only thing to do is wait for them to calm down.

The silent calm of a cypress pond belies the rigors of ranch work in this hot, humid setting. The peninsula on which the Whitehead ranch sits is dotted with many oblong ponds that some original settlers thought were once whale nests. These cypress trees (left) were planted in 1910 by Joe Whitehead's grandfather, Addison.

The last sunlight of the day (above) paints the water a shiny black and the cypress trunks a bronze orange, telling the tale of widely ranging water levels throughout the coastal cattle country. The cypress ponds provide a comforting, deep shade all day long, even at high noon.

THIS TEXAS JUDGE uses a former school for his office. He holds court in the old cafeteria. The crimes are nothing too serious—swiping oysters from a private reef in the bay, stealing a calf for a private barbecue, or occasionally a bit of bodily harm.

Quinten Jackson comes from a prominent Chambers County family. His great-great-granddaddy, Humphrey Jackson, came to the area in 1823 as one of the first white Texans. Quinten wears tight-fitting jeans and scuffed Nocona boots dusted with dry dirt. He always carries a handgun, and his spurs are polished by years of wear. A person in this part of Texas never knows when he'll need his spurs, and Jackson's spurs have spoken to many a high-spirited horse.

The judge wears a wide-brimmed hat but almost always takes it off in his office. He sits with his feet up on his desk next to a framed picture of his handsome son in a football uniform.

Everything in this part of Texas has a lot of space around it. Early land-grant ranches once were more than a hundred miles across. They're not quite as never-ending anymore, but five, twenty, sixty thousand acres of land isn't small either. "Big" in Texas can be, and should be, a birthright, not something to pay a lot of attention to.

Quinten, age sixty-two, is justice of the peace for District 3, a part of Chambers County, Texas. District 3 extends out into Galveston Bay; it has almost as much water as it does land. The land is sand-land and it juts out into the brackish bay like a thumb. On the south side of this thumb of land is East Bay; on the north side, Trinity Bay. Looking west is Galveston Bay, and it's only forty miles to the center of Houston. But while the sand-land and the sprawling city are geographically close, they are about a hundred years apart. And there's no doubt among the sand-land people as to which place is the better world to live in.

Judge Jackson's district stretches east to the Barrows ranch, and takes in the communities of Double Bayou, Smith Point, and Oak Island. If someone drowns in the bay, Judge Jackson presides over the inquest. If there is shooting, Judge Jackson is there. If some lovesick couple "done been fussin' and fightin'" and the relatives are worried maybe they might hurt each other, Quinten goes over and tries to calm everyone down. He calls them by their first names and usually has the angriest one sit down with him while gently suggesting to the other to ease off into the yard and walk around.

Judge Jackson knows about everyone here and what they do. Usually he has a good idea why they misbehave—because Ron lost his job at the auto parts store, because Lucille's not been taking her medication, because Joselle's back to drinkin', and because every couple of years Ricky just has to hit somebody.

One of the cats at the Whitehead ranch waits for some leftovers in the relative comfort behind a screen door.

South Texas Deer

Rarely have I been around wild animals that didn't seem to care if I was there or not. That happened between the Colorado and Caney Rivers, not far north of the Matagorda Peninsula. In bright daylight. Magnificent white-tail bucks, their necks bulging, strutted beneath majestic live oak trees. A hundred feet away, two others smashed their hard antlers together and fought for a doe that was even then in the sights of another high-racked buck.

It was not this way all the time. This was no Garden of Eden, although my Texas friends would argue the point. It was the time of the rut, that one time each year when white-tailed deer mate.

South Texas is home to some of the best deer in North America, thanks to a nutrient-rich soil, gigantic ranches that provide excellent cover, an abundance of water, fields of row crops for feed, and superior genetics. I was privileged to photograph these normally wary deer at a massive ranch near the Caney River in Matagorda County, Texas.

161

This mature doe, very possibly already bred since there was no buck around, feasts on the lush wild grass in the shade of some mature live oaks. *Matagorda County.*

With a countryside like the area to the right to call home, these deer have thrived. The early autumn sunshine illumines this clearing and testifies to why Texans are so proud of the beauty of the place.

I startled these deer and the dominant buck led the does away. *Near Van Vleck.*

The shade of a clump of live oak trees (above) affords this doe and buck some seclusion. A minute later, though, two less dominant bucks, hot on the doe's trail, drove the couple into the open sun and the deep weeds (left), where they paused to check me out again. *Matagorda County.*

I came this way to escape the possible dangers of a hurricane and found a world of deer. The countryside was in full autumnal splendor and the wildlife were oblivious to my intrusion. At times, the area reminded me of Africa, with its open plains, occasional low-spreading massive trees, and humid heat. Everywhere I looked, bucks and does were paired off or pairing off. I was indeed the intruder, but the scene was one as close to perfect as I think I could ever find on earth. *Caney River.*

Seadrift, Texas

T he only reason I came to know anything about Seadrift, Texas, was because I was running out of gas. I was in no mood to stop, look, or listen that day. Instead, I was hungry for the brawny speed and blow-back power of my boat.

The town of Seadrift is between two oceans, one of water, the other of crops. The citizens (population 1,277), however, prefer the water. They draw their livelihood from the unpredictable bays and the Gulf; some are even repelled by the orderliness of the rows of crops.

The people perch here on the edge of these Texas flatlands and don't go inland all that much; instead they roam the waters around their home port. Most return every evening in their modest bay boats to their unassuming homes.

Had I not been low on gas, I not only would have missed Seadrift, I would have missed meeting one of the most outspoken and bravest people I have ever met.

Depending on how good your eyes are, or how foggy it is, or how much you have drunk, you might look at downtown Seadrift and wonder if it's a mirage. There are murals everywhere. A night scene of a shrimp boat washed up on the beach after a wicked storm. Flocks of geese and ducks fly across a wall. It is as if the locals cannot bear to be away from their boats and the natural world, so they bring the outside world into town with them. These murals cover the side walls of the old drugstore, Elena's Restaurant, an insurance agency, and a few other unnamed buildings on Main Street.

During the rush before shrimping season opens (far right), many fishermen find it necessary to stay up late with engine repairs, gear maintenance, or whatever may be needed to be ready at sunrise when the fleet sets out.

As a child, Diane Wilson used to dehead shrimp in the summer to earn a bit of spending money. She was always barefoot, tan, her thick black hair uncombed.

A lone boat heads to port amid storm clouds and biting wind. The water mirrors the sky and seems to unite with it in banishing the shrimpers and fishermen back to land.

IANE WILSON was one of the most determined people I encountered during my journey along the edge of America. She was my age, had five children, and read Faulkner. Diane trusted me with the stories of her growing up in Seadrift.

"It was raining hard," she began. "It was a dark and stormy week. My washing machine was totally broke down. It only breaks down when it's real stormy," Diane laughed.

"I was real hard at work on the laundry when my best friend, Kathy, spotted my car and came in. Luckily she didn't have her kids with her that night. That was probably the one time in our lives we didn't have a pile of kids around.

"Anyway, for as long as I can remember, since I was about ten, I had this reoccurring dream. When I hit thirty-seven I had it every night for weeks. For weeks." Diane wove her story with passion. "It was driving me nuts, and it was a real simple dream.

"In the dream I was always on an isolated beach. On the beach there was a big, solid house . . . but there wasn't any paint on it. It had a weathered look to it, kind of plain. There were a lot of windows that were gleaming and glowing.

"Inside the windows I could see shining furniture, all interesting-looking pieces. Then I would be walking through the entire house, just being amazed at everything that was in the drawers and pulling them out and looking at them. All the precious things of value in those drawers! I still remember the gleam of the windows reflecting off the gleam of the furniture. It was just . . . it was just beautiful. It was beautiful inside.

In the laundromat that night I told Kathy the dream. "She just looked at me real gentle and said, 'Well, the house is yourself. And you're realizing that there are things of worth in the house, in you. You've always thought you were dull and weathered, insignificant, tired. That unpainted house is you, Diane.'

"It was so simple," Diane exclaimed. She told me how she'd suffered with low self-esteem all her life. She repeated that in her childhood home women were considered stupid.

After that night, Diane's life changed. Understanding her dream gave her courage to speak out, to do what she felt was necessary. Now nothing shuts her up; no one can stop her. Today she is making up for decades of imposed silence.

Diane tells people, for instance, that she hears the bays crying. The waters from which four generations of her family have drawn their living are calling out to her for help. And she will not be quiet about it, no matter if some think she's a nut or a foolish, emotional woman.

The heart of Diane's message is that something is dreadfully wrong in her world of saltwater bays. In the past couple of years, black buzzards have begun to stand on the beaches, waiting for death to wash up. The largest dolphin kill in American history from "unknown" causes occurred in these waters, which once enriched Seadrift and filled the nets of its people.

As my journey ended near the Texas-Mexico border, I received this gorgeous sunset as a parting gift from the most fantastic voyage of my life—but certainly not the last. *North of Port Mansfield*.